COLUMBIA BASIN CCC
6739 24th St. - Bldg. 24(
Moses Lake, WA 98837-3

Dyslexia

Elaine Landau

Franklin Watts
A Division of Scholastic Inc.
New York • Toronto • London • Auckland • Sydney
Mexico City • New Delhi • Hong Kong
Danbury, Connecticut

Dedication

For Connie Mirando, a terrific teacher

Cover design by Robert O'Brien.
Interior design by Kathleen Santini.
Graphic p. 28 and on cover reprinted with permission from
 *Reading, Writing, and Speech Problems in Children and Selected
 Papers* by Samuel Torrey Orton, p. 272, courtesy of
 the International Dyslexia Association.

Library of Congress Cataloging-in-Publication Data

Landau, Elaine.
    Dyslexia / by Elaine Landau.
        v. cm. — (Life balance)
    Includes bibliographical references and index.
    Contents: Being dyslexic—Dyslexia—Getting help—Questions
    and answers about dyslexia—Glossary.
        ISBN 0-531-12217-4 (lib. bdg.)   0-531-16612-0 (pbk.)
    1. Dyslexia—Juvenile literature. [1. Dyslexia] I. Title. II. Series.
        RC394.W6L36 2004
        616.85'53—dc21
                                            2003007142

```
a nesst isin aBeg GeeTee
The mother Brd Mad The
ness See poti on the Bdnc
to the Tee amaa the Pheet
Tifz See        twigg
le z an        sof
Raz in        neest
has            t
```

Table of Contents

One

What Is Dyslexia?

Picture this: You are on an airplane with your teachers and classmates taking a trip to Greece. When the plane lands in Athens—the country's capital—everyone is filled with excitement, ready to experience Greek food, culture, and customs. The other students all speak, write, and read Greek. They learned the language early on in school, and their knowledge will serve them well. They visit Athens's restaurants, order whatever they want from the menu, and tell the waiter in Greek how they'd like it cooked. They go to the city's museums and shops, mixing with the local people. They enjoy an evening of Greek theater as well. The students easily do what's expected of them, and they make it all seem so simple.

While your classmates enjoy themselves, your experiences in Greece differ sharply. Like your classmates, you tried to learn Greek. You had the same teachers, used the same textbooks, and sat in the same classrooms. But Greek didn't come easily to you. It wasn't for lack of trying. Sometimes you worked at it considerably longer and harder than some of your classmates who now speak it fluently. But you only picked up bits and pieces of the language. It was sometimes difficult for you to distinguish some words from others. Stringing the words together to make meaningful sentences and paragraphs was a challenge as well.

There were times when you thought you were making some progress, but it took you much longer than the other students to read in Greek. They tired of listening to you try to read in class. When they weren't laughing, they were bored waiting for you to finish stumbling over the words. It wasn't long before your turn to read became a cue for them to turn to one another and start talking.

Sometimes you feel about ready to give up. Once the rest of the class mastered the Greek basics, they moved ahead at a fast pace. Before long they were reading whole books in that language and doing lengthy book reports. They even read Greek books when they didn't have to.

All this has caused you to seriously doubt yourself. Why didn't you pick up Greek as easily as the rest of the class? You had been friends with these kids since preschool, and then they hadn't seemed smarter than you. Now it's as if they've left you in the dust. They've separated themselves from you in other ways as well. Lots of them have called you "stupid." You've even turned around a few times when you heard the word "retard" called out.

You desperately want to be like everyone else, but this Greek thing has become a barrier. You've tried to find a way around it, but it's hard. The Greek taught at your school is a foundation for other subjects. If you don't catch up soon, you are likely to fall behind in other areas as well. You feel isolated and cut off from just about everyone.

Being in a foreign country and not knowing the language can certainly make you feel out of the loop. But what if you were in your own country and had trouble reading and writing the only language you've ever known? Undoubtedly, that would be even worse. Nevertheless, that situation is what some young people with dyslexia face every day.

What Is Dyslexia?

Dyslexia is a type of learning disability. It usually affects a person's ability to read, write, and spell. A young person who can't learn to read around the same time other children do may be thought of as dumb. Yet people with dyslexia are often quite intelligent—some are even gifted. Individuals with dyslexia can also be extremely creative and resourceful. They are highly visual and tend to think in pictures. These pictures are three-dimensional, like a computer graphic. The ability to look at things this way is often considered a talent and is highly valued in such professions as architecture and art. However, these strong points are rarely obvious when a young person with dyslexia is trying to learn basic skills such as reading and writing.

Individuals with dyslexia are highly visual and tend to think in pictures. The ability to look at things this way is highly valued in such professions as architecture and art.

Dyslexia was first recognized as a learning difficulty in England in 1896. A doctor named James Kerr who worked in the school system noticed that some children with perfect vision were still unable to read words. Therefore, he called the problem *word blindness.* This term is still sometimes used today in Britain as well as in parts of Scandinavia. Karl Kussman, a German professor, was the first person to actually label the disorder *dyslexia.* In Greek, the term *dys* means "difficulty" and *lexis* means "word" or "language."

In the mid-1920s, Dr. Samuel T. Orton, a psychiatrist and neuropathologist (a doctor who diagnoses diseases of the nervous system through the microscopic examination of human tissue), became interested in dyslexia. He was especially curious about one teenager who scored extremely well on nonverbal tests (tests without words) but who could barely read. Orton, along with psychologist Anna Gillingham, devised a multisensory method (a technique that combines seeing the word, hearing the word, and writing the word) to help dyslexic students with their language skills. Their method, known as the Orton-Gillingham approach, as well as similar methods based on it continues to be used in many schools today.

It is currently estimated that about 5 to 20 percent of school-age children are affected to some degree by dyslexia. People with dyslexia can be found at every intelligence level, though it's sometimes difficult to measure their level using standard intelligence tests in a classroom setting. Often such tests do not truly measure their abilities. That's because students taking the test have to read and respond to a series of questions. Since many people with dyslexia do not read, write, or spell well, they typically tend to get low scores on these exams.

However, when the testing situations are especially adapted to the learning style of persons with dyslexia, there's often a significant improvement in scores. In such situations, students with dyslexia are usually tested individually rather than with a group. The questions are asked orally, or extra time is allotted for them to read the test material. Their answers are sometimes allowed to be given orally as well.

Family Ties

While there are many people with dyslexia throughout the world, dyslexia is not contagious. No one can "catch" this learning disability from a friend or a sibling. Dyslexia is found in both rich and poor people and among people of all races and religions. It also has nothing to do with poor parenting, a bad home environment, or laziness or stupidity.

Instead, dyslexia appears to be largely an inherited condition. There is scientific evidence to indicate that genetics is a factor in this disorder. Genes are present in the cells of all living things and are passed down from parents to their children. Genes determine how we look and the way we grow, and influence some of the conditions or disorders we are prone to. Researchers have found that dyslexia seems to be passed down in families through the generations.

There is scientific evidence to indicate that genetics is a factor in this disorder.

That doesn't mean that everyone related to someone with dyslexia will also have this learning disability. Some family members may and some may not. This is true even in cases of identical twins. In studying dyslexia in identical twins, researchers found that in approximately half the sets of twins, both twins had developed dyslexia. Among the other half, only one twin had this learning disability.

The Gender Factor

While at one time it was thought that dyslexia was more common in boys than in girls, researchers no longer believe this is true. However, boys are still more often tested and treated for the disorder than girls.

There is no cure for dyslexia, and no one outgrows this learning disability. Dyslexia does not fade away with age. Research shows that nearly 75 percent of first graders who experience reading problems will be poor readers in high school if they don't receive help. Yet with proper instruction and hard work, people with dyslexia often excel in many areas of life.

Learning Disability or Learning Difference?

While dyslexia is often referred to as a learning disability, many people object to that label. They feel the word "disability" implies that the person cannot learn or has a problem learning. Some educators strongly disagree with this view of dyslexia. They stress that the problem isn't that people with dyslexia can't learn—they just can't learn through the standard instructional methods used to teach the majority of children.

Individuals with dyslexia learn differently than most people and must be taught differently in order to overcome the difference. That's why it's sometimes argued that dyslexia should be called a "learning difference" instead of

Success Stories

Many individuals with dyslexia have overcome the obstacles in their way. Some even became rich and famous. A few well-known people with dyslexia are:

Tom Cruise	*Walt Disney*
Harry Belafonte	*Greg Louganis*
Richard Chamberlain	*Winston Churchill*
Bruce Jenner	*Vincent van Gogh*
Danny Glover	*Woodrow Wilson*
Cher	*Alexander Graham Bell*
Jay Leno	*Julius Caesar*
Albert Einstein	*Whoopi Goldberg*
Henry Winkler	*Nolan Ryan*
Leonardo da Vinci	*Magic Johnson*

a "learning disability." Regardless of what it is called, if dyslexia isn't recognized and treated early on, it's likely that a young person with dyslexia will be headed down a rocky road.

It's sometimes argued that dyslexia should be called a "learning difference" instead of a "learning disability."

Nevertheless, a rocky road does not mean a roadblock. This country is filled with people with dyslexia who have distinguished themselves. They overcame the obstacles in their way and served as an example to others. One such individual is Charles Schwab. Schwab, the founder of one of the most successful investment firms in the nation, has been hailed by many as a financial genius. Schwab is the recipient of a good deal of praise today, but things were very different for him growing up. For years, he struggled to meet the rigid requirements of an unyielding school system. He didn't know what was wrong, but he had always had a hard time with reading and memorization—two skills that were vital to success in school.

In high school, Schwab read comic books because the classics were well beyond him. Though his Scholastic Aptitude Test (SAT) scores were low, he was still admitted to Stanford University in the 1950s. It wasn't long, however,

Learning Disabilities and Related Conditions

Even extremely bright and creative people can have a learning problem that makes it difficult for them to acquire basic academic skills. Dyslexia is not the only learning disability. Here are a few of the most common disabilities that can also affect learning:

Dyscalculia

Dyscalculia is a term used to describe a range of learning disabilities that are related to math. The difficulties that arise with dyscalculia vary from person to person and often surface as math becomes an increasingly important part of the curriculum. Some students with this learning disability have trouble remembering basic math facts. For example, they may find that it takes them much longer than their classmates to learn the time tables, and even after memorizing them, they frequently mix up or forget some of the numbers.

Students with dyscalculia also often have difficulty with the sequence of steps needed to complete a math problem. They frequently leave out a step or do not do the steps in the proper order. This can be especially troublesome in the more advanced grades, where multistep procedures are common.

Dyspraxia

Dyspraxia is a disorder that affects motor skills development (movement) and, in turn, can negatively influence various aspects of learning and school performance. As the National Center for Learning Disabilities says of this disorder, "Dyspraxia can affect different areas of functioning, varying from simple motor tasks such as waving goodbye to more complex tasks …" Young people with dyspraxia often have a poor sense of direction, difficulties with handwriting, and speech delays. The disorder can affect a student's performance in subjects where writing and speech are essential.

Information processing disorders

Information processing disorders are conditions in which people have difficulty effectively using the information they collect through their senses. While information processing disorders are not regarded as specific learning disabilities, they are frequently present in individuals who have learning disabilities. The National Center for Learning Disabilities stresses that these disorders "can often explain why a person is having trouble with learning and performance."

Among school-age children, information processing disorders sometimes interfere with their ability to remember names and directions. It may also be difficult for these students to recall the items on even a short list or to understand some-one who tends to speak quickly.

Any learning disability or related problem can make school harder for students and can undermine their confidence. However, when these young people receive proper help, there is often tremendous improvement.

before Schwab began failing English at Stanford. Looking back, he describes the experience as "devastating." Although he didn't know it, there was a reason for this brilliant man's failure in high school and college: Schwab had dyslexia.

Schwab was later able to turn things around and fulfill his potential. He shined in the financial world, where the kind of creative thinking people with dyslexia are known for worked to his advantage. Amazingly, Schwab didn't know he had dyslexia until the 1980s, when one of his five children was diagnosed with the disorder. He recognized his child's symptoms in himself and that answered many of the questions he had always wondered about.

Today, Schwab is determined to help young people with dyslexia. In 1988, he and his wife Helen started the Schwab Foundation for Learning. The foundation gives the parents of children with dyslexia the information they need to help their children have the best lives and make the most of who they are.

Another case in point is that of the Emmy Award-winning writer-producer and best-selling author Stephen J. Cannell. Cannell has enjoyed a spectacularly successful career writing books as well as scripts for television and film, but he hardly had a typical start as a writer. Graduating at the bottom of his high-school class, Cannell noted that his goal of becoming an author was "a very cocky idea for a guy who couldn't pass most of his English courses." Undaunted by his poor academic performance, Cannell still listed "author" as his ambition in his high school yearbook.

Cannell is exceptionally smart but has fought severe dyslexia, which remained undiagnosed during his high-school years. Besides being an outstanding writer, Cannell has also proved to be an able businessman. He began his own independent production company and has done quite well.

Like Schwab, Cannell has worked to help others with dyslexia. He speaks publicly about this learning disability, which helps to increase awareness. He has also sponsored and performed in a filmed play about famous people with dyslexia called *Gifts of Greatness*.

Understanding
Two
Dyslexia

You put your right foot in
You put your right foot out
You put your right foot in and
You shake it all about.
You do the Hokey Pokey and
You turn yourself around.
That's what it's all about!

The Hokey Pokey is a favorite children's song and dance that preschoolers across the country eagerly look forward to. For most of them, the Hokey Pokey offers a time to sing, shake their limbs, and smile. But for someone with dyslexia, it can be a highly frustrating exercise. That's because many people with dyslexia have difficulty telling right from left.

Fourteen-year-old Katy, who was an assistant at her church's preschool, loved working with young children but hated the Hokey Pokey. Katy is dyslexic, and while she can tell left from right, it takes her longer than most people to figure it out. Katy can easily handle this if she's alone following directions, but if a bunch of small children are looking to her to lead a game, she becomes frustrated. That's why Katy made sure she wasn't around when the preschool class did the Hokey Pokey every Sunday. She'd have to go to the restroom, call home, or come up with something else to ensure that she wasn't available when the children formed the circle for the dance.

One Sunday, Katy returned from the restroom to find that the children hadn't finished the Hokey Pokey as she had anticipated but instead were waiting for her to lead the group. There was no escape. She suggested they try Ring around the Rosie or Here We Go 'round the Mulberry Bush, but her ploy didn't work—the children insisted on doing the Hokey Pokey. Katy started off by putting her left foot in the circle instead of her right. At first it looked like none of the children would notice, until one precocious little boy called out, "Hey, stop! Katy's doing it all wrong."

Having been through similar situations before, Katy quickly answered, "Just checking to see how alert you are.

I wondered if you'd catch my mistake. Let's finish the Hokey Pokey using any of our arms and legs. Right or left doesn't matter today." To her relief, Katy got away with it. The children didn't realize that she had trouble telling her right from her left.

Nevertheless, Katy was upset over the incident. She realized that she had only been able to pull it off because she was dealing with three and four year olds. Katy thought how awful it would be if the church congregation found out about her problem. She felt sure that everyone would think she was stupid. Even though Katy was just fourteen she felt as if she'd been keeping her secret forever. Katy was tired of pretending, but she believed she had no choice.

The Science of Dyslexia

Young people who have dyslexia often spend a good deal of time wondering what's wrong with them. At the present time, we don't have all the answers. The National Institute of Neurological Disorders and Stroke describes dyslexia as being "brain-based." While much more research in this area is needed, many scientists think there are some differences in how the brains of people with dyslexia develop and work. Some research points to the fact that individuals with dyslexia may experience problems processing sounds in their brains. Scientists at the University of California at San Francisco found that people with dyslexia have difficulty trying to link certain consonants such as *b* and *d* to specific letters.

The National Institute of Neurological Disorders and Stroke describes dyslexia as being "brain-based." Many scientists think there are some differences in how the brains of people with dyslexia develop and work.

Researchers have also studied dyslexia using a variety of scans and imaging techniques to show how different parts of the brain work during specific tasks. They've learned a great deal with the help of functional magnetic resonance imaging (fmri), a high-tech scan that allows researchers to see which portions of the brain receive the most blood at any given time. This increased blood flow indicates increased activity in that part of the brain.

Scientists have long known that the left side of the brain is concerned with processing language. With functional magnetic reasoning imaging, they can break down the process even more. By studying the blood-flow patterns in the brains of children as they read, scientists learned that three specific regions in the brain's left hemisphere are crucial to reading. These three regions work together to allow the brain to link letters to sounds, recognize different sounds, and immediately identify familiar words. In people with dyslexia, however, the process encounters a glitch. Their brain scans suggest that they have trouble linking the sound to the letter as well as instantly recognizing familiar words. This, in turn, leads to reading problems.

As Yale neuroscientist and leading researcher Dr. Sally Shaywitz, noted, "The good news [associated with this research] is that we really understand the steps of how you become a reader and how you become a skilled reader." Therefore, programs that are specifically tailored to helping children with dyslexia to strengthen these weak areas can be further developed. So far, among the most successful programs in this realm are those that stress linking letters to sounds.

The research also hints at a very exciting possibility. In some cases, if children receive the right type of instruction early enough, their brains may become so completely rewired that they are no longer dyslexic. While this has not been conclusively proven, Dr. Shaywitz noted some important changes in the brain scans of kindergarten and first grade children exhibiting dyslexic symptoms after they received help. Once they'd completed a full year of intensive targeted instruction, their brain scans began to look very much like those of children who did not have dyslexia.

The Dyslexic Experience

All people with dyslexia are not alike. People tend to experience the disorder differently. In severe cases, a person may be unable to read or write a simple sentence. Other people who are dyslexic just have a problem spelling. However, the majority of people with dyslexia have trouble decoding or processing language. They have difficulty making the connection between the sound and the letter that represents that sound. It is hard for them to break down words into the smallest units of sound known as phonemes. Yet phonetics (the process of sounding out words) is usually a key factor in learning to read.

Large numbers of people with dyslexia also have trouble remembering whole words. If the teacher gives the class some vocabulary words to learn, a person with dyslexia will usually have a much harder time remembering them than other students. Even if the student with dyslexia learns the words, that individual will often have difficulty recognizing the same words when they are used later in sentences and paragraphs. At times, a student with dyslexia may recognize a word in a book but if the same word is used differently in the next chapter, he or she may not know it.

It isn't just whole words that present problems for people with dyslexia. The trouble exists with letters as well. Large numbers of these individuals have difficulty remembering the individual letters within words. Letters that look somewhat alike—like *b* and *d* or *q* and *p*—can be an added source of frustration. To get an idea of what it's like for a person with dyslexia to read a page, hold a book up to a mirror and try reading it. Are you able to do it? If so, can you read as quickly as you usually do? People with dyslexia deal with a similar experience whenever they pick up a book, a magazine, or even a restaurant menu.

English Isn't Easy

There are more than 1,100 ways that letters are used to symbolize the forty sounds in the English language. With a less complex language, such as Italian, children with dyslexia have an easier time learning to read. Although dyslexia is found throughout the world, at least one study has revealed that there are twice as many people identified with dyslexia in English-speaking cultures as in countries where simpler languages are spoken.

Speech

Some people with dyslexia have trouble with speech as well as with reading and writing. It's hard for them to find the right words to express themselves. These individuals also have difficulty understanding complex explanations given by others. It's almost as if the words get in the way. One highly intelligent young man with dyslexia recalls that when he was in nursery school, he was quite a talker. He enthusiastically spoke all the time, telling his classmates and teachers all about his pets and family trips. The trouble was, however, that no one understood what he was saying. His words simply didn't make sense.

At the same time, the reverse can be true for other people with dyslexia. While they may have difficulty reading and writing, their speech is unaffected. In fact, many of these individuals speak beautifully. This was true for Shawn, a young man with dyslexia who expressed his thoughts so well that he became one of his high school's top debaters. Shawn was a natural at public speaking. The spoken word came easily to him, and his debating points were always well taken and crystal clear. Known for his enthusiasm when verbally battling an opponent, Shawn remained consistently effective even in front of large audiences.

Shawn was envied by many of those who heard him speak and saw his debating club trophies. Yet things were different when Shawn had to express his thoughts in a written paragraph. Here, he had to struggle just to make himself understood. Reading had never been easy for Shawn, either. Even after receiving help for his dyslexia, he read more slowly than other students and had to work much harder at it. Shawn sometimes had to read something two or three times just to get the gist of it, but if someone said the same thing to him, he immediately understood it.

Dyslexic Dysgraphia

People with dyslexia who have trouble writing have a condition known as dyslexic dysgraphia. Writing is an extremely difficult task for these individuals. It sometimes takes a great deal of concentration and energy for them just to remember where on the paper to put their pencil back down when writing a sentence. With dyslexic dysgraphia, the individual's penmanship can be hard to decipher.

Better at Painting than Penmanship

You might expect a famous painter's handwriting to be flawless, but everyone had trouble reading whatever the acclaimed Italian painter Leonardo da Vinci wrote. After studying the artist's notes and manuscripts, scientists concluded that he had dyslexia. Da Vinci wrote backward from right to left, in a mirror image. Spelling errors and other dyslexic-like language difficulties were identified as well. Despite this obstacle, da Vinci became one of the world's greatest artists.

Often the letters are not properly formed. At times, these individuals write their letters and even their words backward. Frequently, their handwriting is very small and may not stay on a straight line. The words sometimes trail off the page. A random mixture of upper- and lower-case letters may be used as well.

Sometimes just mastering the basic mechanics of writing can distract students with dyslexia from the subject they

A nesr is in a big tree The mother bird made Ine nest
She Put it on The branch of The Tree among The
Pretty leaves She made it oft wigs leaves and grass
She pur Soft rags inside of it The nest naS five Doby
birds init

anesst iS in a Reg Gee Tee The morher Brd mad
The ness See poti on The Banc to The Tee
a m a a The Pne er rifz See mad it of Twigg
Le z and gas See put Sof Ra z in sidofit
The nevst has fife Baby Brdint

The above writing samples, written by a child with dyslexia, show the contrast between copying and writing to dictation. The top paragraph was copied from an existing document. The bottom paragraph was written from dictation.

set out to write about. As might be expected, it often takes students with dyslexia considerably longer than their classmates to write a paragraph. This can be a problem when completing assignments in class or when taking tests. It is also difficult when students only have a few minutes to copy their homework assignments off the board before the bell rings and still get to their next class on time.

It often takes students with dyslexia considerably longer than their classmates to write a paragraph. This can be a problem when completing assignments in class or when taking tests.

This became a serious dilemma for Jim even though he was only mildly affected by dyslexia. Because Jim's dyslexia symptoms were slight, he had never been diagnosed during elementary school. Though not an outstanding student, no one ever thought of Jim as learning disabled. He had always managed to keep up with his class and was known to be conscientious and hard-working. Through the years, Jim hadn't realized that he was actually working harder than most of the other students to earn the same or even lower grades. He was simply used to doing what he needed to do.

The type of elementary school Jim attended had been helpful as well. It was a small private school where students were encouraged to work at their own pace. There were usually no more than twelve students in a class and they learned in a relaxed atmosphere. Speed was not considered as important as comprehension, and this had worked to Jim's advantage.

Everything changed after graduation, however, when Jim entered a large public junior high school. Now Jim had six subjects with six different teachers. There was a lot of material to cover, and there never seemed to be enough time to finish it. Students were required to copy their homework assignments from the board in less than three minutes. Jim found that nearly impossible to do. He had only written the first few words of what was on the board by the time his classmates were already out the door and down the hall.

When Jim got home at the end of the day, the few notes he'd been able to jot down were illegible. He tried to rely on his memory to complete his assignments but that had disastrous effects. Since junior high was more challenging than elementary school had been, Jim was already trying harder than ever, but he was still falling behind in his work. His parents and teachers thought that Jim's declining grades might have to do with the adjustment of going from a small school to a larger one. After one of his teachers observed the difficulty Jim was having copying things off the board, however, he was tested to see what was wrong. The tests made everything clear for Jim, his teachers, and his parents. They revealed that Jim had dyslexia.

Math

While most people associate dyslexia with problems in reading, writing, or speech, some people with dyslexia do quite well in these areas. Instead, they have trouble with math. This may be because, in a way, math is a language, too. The numbers are symbols in the same way that the letters of the alphabet are. Just as people with dyslexia who have trouble reading may reverse their letters, those struggling with math often do the same with numbers. For example, they may write the number 812 when they really meant to write 821.

The brilliant, though dyslexic, scientist and inventor Thomas Edison had this problem. Unable to meet his teachers' expectations, he was thrown out of school when he was just twelve years old. His worst subject was math, which his teachers claimed he wasn't focusing on. His schooltime struggle with numbers, nevertheless, didn't stop him from patenting more than one thousand inventions later in life.

Overcoming Odds

Polar explorer Ann Bancroft found her life filled with challenges early on. As a young girl, she had been fascinated by the story of Ernest Shackleton's daring 1914 antarctic expedition and dreamed of one day making the journey herself. However, Bancroft had her own obstacles to overcome. School had always been a frustrating experience for Bancroft, who was diagnosed with dyslexia in the seventh grade.

Despite her condition, Bancroft went on to carve out a special life for herself. After graduating from college, she became a physical education teacher. She also worked as an instructor for a wilderness program that helped both disabled and able-bodied people enjoy the great outdoors. Yet Bancroft longed to do some of the exciting things she had read about as a child. She refused to let dyslexia stop her from achieving her goals.

Bancroft set off on her first polar expedition in 1986 and became the first woman to reach the North Pole by dogsled. That was just the start of things to come. Bancroft later led an expedition of four women across Antarctica, and on January 14, 1993, she became the first woman to have reached both the North and South Poles. Bancroft is a shining example of what people can achieve if they set their minds to it.

Social Skills

Besides finding their schoolwork difficult, some students with dyslexia may, at times, be less adept in social situations than other children their age. This occurs because children with dyslexia sometimes mature a bit more slowly. This, however, does not put them at a permanent disadvantage. These young people can easily be taught appropriate reactions in social situations, and parents can work with them to further enhance their social skills. Counseling and behavioral therapy are frequently useful, as well.

Organizational Skills

Problems with reading, writing, spelling, speaking, or math can be daunting. Yet all these difficulties are worsened if the individual is poorly organized. Unfortunately, many people with dyslexia have poor organizational skills. Studying for exams takes effort, and knowing what to study as well as where the necessary books and papers are is crucial. Misplacing key course assignments or mixing together notes from several subjects can undermine hours of serious study and any reasonable plan for success. Since people with dyslexia often have problems getting organized, it is essential for them to work harder in this area. It can sometimes make the difference between a passing grade and a failing one.

Many people with dyslexia have poor organizational skills. Misplacing key course assignments or mixing together notes from several subjects can undermine hours of serious study and any reasonable plan for success.

Dyslexia and Coordination

Some people with dyslexia have difficulty with balance and coordination. As a result, sports can be another challenging area for people with dyslexia. At times, individuals who have found schoolwork difficult have shined on the athletic field. While this may be true for some people with dyslexia, others have poor coordination. This can make it hard to excel at baseball, basketball, volleyball, soccer, and other team sports.

It can also put doing detailed handicraft projects out of reach. That's how it was for Lena, a young girl with dyslexia, who came from a family of expert embroiderers. Her grandmother, mother, two aunts, and older sister created beautiful and elaborate embroidery on tablecloths, napkins, and bed linens. Over the years, it had become a family hobby of sorts. At times, the women followed patterns, but they also took pride in creating their own intricate and highly detailed designs.

Lena had tried embroidery many times, but because it required precision and exacting handiwork, she found it more frustrating than pleasurable. The women all looked forward to their embroidery sessions at family get-togethers, and Lena began to feel left out. Her mother tried to help by finding simple patterns for Lena to work on, but her work still looked sloppy, which proved to be a source of stress for Lena.

In the end, Lena did what many people with dyslexia learn to do when faced with obstacles: she compensated. Lena found a way to replace something she could do well for the activity that had presented the problem. Since Lena was an excellent photographer, she began videotaping her family's embroidery sessions. She also interviewed each of the women involved, asking them to explain how they felt about their embroidery and why they thought it had become part of their family's heritage. The project was worthwhile and was ideal for Lena. Because her subjects' answers were taped, she was spared the task of having to write down what everyone said.

The series of tapes took about a year to complete. After that, the photography teacher at her school helped Lena edit the work. The end result was a moving oral history of the women in her family. With her teacher's help, Lena's tapes were entered in a contest for young filmmakers

The Path to Success

Paul Orfalea is the founder of Kinko's, an international chain of more than one thousand stores. As a child, few would have guessed that he'd have such great success in business. That's because Orfalea is dyslexic, but he was not diagnosed when he was young. Some of his teachers simply thought that he wasn't bright, while others felt he was lazy and reluctant to try. Orfalea was both left back and expelled at various times. Once, he was even admitted to a special school for the mentally retarded. One of his teachers told Orfalea's parents to try to get their son into a decent technical school. The teacher, who meant well, hoped that might lead to a good job for Orfalea in carpet installation following graduation.

Orfalea wanted more for himself. Despite his learning disability, he managed to graduate from high school with a low D average. From there, he went on to the University of Southern California. With a great deal of effort, he made it through the university as well, even though he could hardly read.

By 1970, Orfalea was ready to become the businessman he somehow always knew he could be. His first step was to open a small copying shop, which he ran out of an old hamburger stand. That was the beginning of Kinko's— a business that grew into a multimillion-dollar corporation under Orfalea's direction.

sponsored by a local television station. To her surprise and delight, Lena won second prize. Her work was also shown on a local cable channel. Lena realized that she had accomplished something positive. Rather than remain upset about not being able to embroider well, she had found something else enjoyable at which she excelled.

No matter how a person is affected by dyslexia, he or she can overcome it. The first step, however, is making a diagnosis. A learning disability may be suspected when a young person struggles with basic academic skills, such as reading, writing, or spelling, but tests can help to uncover the problem, as discussed in the following chapter.

Three

Diagnosing Dyslexia

As a young girl, Fannie Flagg knew she wanted to become a writer, but her teachers continually discouraged her. Flagg, undiagnosed at the time, was a terrible speller, and her teachers didn't believe she was capable of becoming a novelist. Though deep inside Flagg felt that she could do it, her teachers' reactions caused her to have some serious self-doubt.

In sixth grade, Flagg's self-confidence was reawakened. One of her teachers told her that she thought Flagg was quite a good speaker. Flagg reasoned that if she could speak well she could probably write well, too. She later went on to do just that, creating such best-sellers as *Fried Green Tomatoes at the Whistle Stop Cafe.* Flagg also took up acting and starred in productions both on Broadway and on television. Today, she is a best-selling author and actress.

Although she'd always had a spelling problem, Flagg did not know she was dyslexic until 1978, when she appeared on a TV game show called the *Match Game.* While on the show, Flagg had to write down her answers, and she continually spelled the answers incorrectly. One day, a teacher who had been watching the show wrote to congratulate Flagg on her success in life despite the fact that she was dyslexic. Flagg was shocked; she had no idea that dyslexia might have been her problem all along. She went for tests, which confirmed

Flagg did not know she was dyslexic until 1978, when she appeared on a TV game show called the Match Game.

the teacher's suspicion. After many years of struggling, Flagg finally knew that her problem had a name. For most of her life, she says, "I just thought I was dumb."

Another famous show-business personality who had to deal with dyslexia is the comedian and late-night talk-show host Jay Leno. Due to dyslexia, Leno had been unable to get the high grades he had hoped for in high school. After graduating with mostly Cs and Ds, Leno, not surprisingly, was denied admission to the college of his choice—Emerson College in Boston, Massachusetts.

Despite the initial rejection, Leno refused to give up. He did everything he could to let the officials at Emerson know that he belonged there. This included sitting outside the admissions office for twelve hours a day, five days a week, until he convinced those in charge to change their minds.

Leno did everything he could to let the officials at Emerson know that he belonged there.

Leno's success shows that, in the end, the college made the right choice in admitting him. In addition to his abundant talent, his determination and perseverance has

Early Signs of Dyslexia
While dyslexia is frequently identified in school-age children, there may be early warning signs even in younger children. These preschoolers may have difficulty:
- *using scissors or crayons*
- *being understood by people outside the family circle*
- *buttoning or zipping up clothing*
- *remembering the letters of the alphabet*
- *following simple directions*
- *remembering or recognizing rhymes*

helped Leno get where he is today. He credits having dyslexia with helping him to develop these qualities.

Milder cases of dyslexia are not always present early on. These individuals don't have much of a problem reading and spelling simple words. As their language needs become more complex, however, things become more difficult for them. In some cases, people with dyslexia will confuse words that sound the same. If you showed persons with dyslexia a tomato and asked them to write down what it is, they might write the word "potato." Yet if you asked them to describe the food, they would be able to tell you that it's a red, round, juicy fruit high in vitamin C. This shows that even though people with dyslexia may clearly know what a tomato is, they may not be able to find the right word for it.

Some common signs of dyslexia include:
- reading slowly and often inaccurately
- avoiding tasks that involve a substantial amount of reading and writing
- experiencing problems in summarizing or outlining materials from textbooks
- exhibiting poor planning and organizational skills
- ignoring details or focusing on them too much
- spelling words incorrectly or spelling the same word different ways within the same piece of writing

- having difficulty filling out forms
- having below-average memory skills for facts, sequences, and information

Testing for Dyslexia

Years ago, there wasn't much help available for people with dyslexia. Not much was known about learning disabilities. If a student didn't do well, parents were usually told that their child simply wasn't smart. Often, the school system urged them to guide the young person toward a job that didn't require a good deal of thinking or a high intellect.

Today, fewer children with dyslexia remain undiagnosed. Educators know a lot more about learning disabilities. They have become fairly sophisticated about spotting these problems in young people and coming up with helpful solutions. When a young student consistently has difficulty in school, testing by a school psychologist or other appropriate professional may be necessary to identify the problem.

Before being tested for learning disabilities, the child's eyesight and hearing may also be evaluated. It is important to rule out possible problems in these areas first. Young children as well as older ones can be tested for dyslexia; testing procedures vary according to the child's age. Because no single test pinpoints this disorder, a series of

Determining the Problem

Students encounter difficulties in school for many reasons. The obstacle may not always be dyslexia. There are two types of tests commonly used to find out more about why a child might be having learning problems: screening tests and comprehensive tests.

Screening Tests

Screening tests are broad-based general tests used with large groups of students who appear to be having difficulty academically. These tests are not specifically designed to pinpoint dyslexia; they instead help zero in on the children who could benefit from more extensive testing for this learning disability.

Screening tests usually ask the students to answer a series of short questions regarding their school performance and feelings about school. Some typical questions might be:

- Are you having trouble learning your weekly spelling words?

- Is it difficult for you to tell left from right?

- Are directions usually confusing to you?

- Is math especially difficult for you?

- Do you dislike the time you spend in school?

Comprehensive Tests

Comprehensive tests are designed to specifically identify any learning disabilities affecting the young person's performance. A series of tests are given to precisely determine the difficulties the child may have in reading, math, spelling, and other areas. The testing is usually done by a psychologist who works with the student on an individual basis and who later compiles a report containing the results. The report will detail the problem at hand and recommend ways that the young person might best be helped.

tests is administered. This type of testing can take from three to six hours and focuses on finding the precise nature and extent of the problem. When younger children are tested, it is often done in two separate sessions. Besides identifying dyslexia, these tests can also reveal the individual's strengths and weaknesses. Such information frequently proves helpful in devising an appropriate educational plan for that person.

Through testing, it might be learned that the student could benefit from having a tutor or by being placed in a special class with other young people working at a similar level. Children with dyslexia tend to do best in a predictable and highly structured classroom setting. Ideally, class size should be small and the learning environment should remain constant; students should know what to expect, with basic routines established and followed daily. Students with dyslexia—as well as many other young people—usually profit from having the material broken down into its simplest parts; from there, they can learn it step-by-step.

It is essential that all students with dyslexia be identified and given the help they need. Otherwise, these young people can too easily fall through the cracks. That's what nearly happened to Kevin, a young man with dyslexia who had struggled a long time with reading. Undiagnosed, Kevin spent much of his time finding ways to get by in school. Real learning had become secondary. "When it came time to do a book report in high school, I turned to shortcuts," he recalled. "I'd read the title page, the back cover, the chapter headings. From there, I'd let my imagination take over."

Kevin managed to maintain a B average through much of high school. But the teenager's strategy fell apart in his junior year, when his parents decided to enroll him in a difficult college-prep school. The new school's standards were considerably higher, and it wasn't long before Kevin's report card was covered with Ds and Fs.

"I guess things kind of caught up with me," Kevin later admitted. "I went from being what teachers call a bright kid to a troubled kid to a lazy kid to a kid who was no longer motivated. I stopped caring." For a while, Kevin's future seemed somewhat uncertain, but after being tested, he got the help he needed to go on to college.

Unfortunately, the same wasn't true for Jack, another young student with dyslexia. By the time Jack entered junior high, he knew he had a problem, but he was too ashamed to admit it or to cooperate with people who tried to help him. Through the years, Jack had tried every imaginable way to get out of doing his work at school. Often, he'd take on the role of class clown. That usually landed him in the principal's office, but at least he wasn't asked to read there. As he got older, Jack pretended that he wasn't interested in

Dying for Success

In recent years, suicide among young people has become a national problem. Thousands of American teenagers take their own lives every year. The American Academy of Child and Adolescent Psychiatry states that suicide is currently the third major cause of death among people from fifteen to twenty-four years old as well as the sixth leading cause of death for five to fourteen year olds.

The organization further notes that "Teenagers experience strong feelings of stress, confusion, self-doubt, pressure to succeed, financial uncertainty and other fears while growing up. For some teenagers, divorce, the formation of a new family with step-parents and step-siblings, or moving to a new community can be very unsettling and can intensify self-doubts. In some cases, suicide appears to be a 'solution.'"

The situation can be even worse for youths with dyslexia. A recent study presented at the American Association of Suicidology in Bethesda, Maryland, revealed that teenagers with dyslexia were more likely to both think about and to attempt suicide than other young people their age. In the study, researchers compared ninety-four students with reading problems to the same number of students who were good readers. Nineteen percent of the students with dyslexia had a history of suicidal thoughts or attempts compared to only 5 percent of the other readers. The researchers further found that the students with dyslexia were ten percent more likely to drop out of school. There was also a strong connection between school dropout rates and suicidal thoughts.

These findings may be at least partly due to the importance of school success during adolescence. Dr. David Goldston, the head researcher in the study, noted that poor academic performance "raises questions about whether they [teens with dyslexia] are going to finish school or what they are going to do after they finish school—what kinds of jobs they are going to get."

Educators evaluating the study stress that it underscores the need for early intervention. The sooner children with dyslexia are diagnosed and helped, the brighter their prospects are.

reading or anything to do with school. It didn't take him long to find friends who felt the same way. Many days, they'd cut classes together or not show up for school at all.

Guaranteed by Law

Young people with dyslexia are entitled by law to a fair and equal public education. That means that public schools must accommodate their special needs. Their rights are protected by the following laws:

- Individuals with Disabilities Education Act (IDEA) of 1997. *This law guarantees the rights of learning-disabled students to receive special education. IDEA provides for an individualized education program to be drawn up for every student with dyslexia. These programs are special-education plans specifically geared to each student's needs.*

- Section 504 of the Rehabilitation Act of 1973 (PL 93–112). *This law prohibits discrimination against students with dyslexia. It guarantees that they will have equal access to programs and services in schools, colleges, and other institutions that receive federal funding.*

- Americans with Disabilities Act (ADA) of 1990. *This law protects people with dyslexia from discrimination in all public and most private schools, testing institutions, and licensing authorities.*

In time, Jack became so disruptive that his behavioral problems overshadowed his learning difficulties. Most of his interactions with his teachers and other school personnel became focused on his poor attitude and rule-breaking antics. When he was just sixteen, Jack dropped out of high school. Sadly, Jack's is not an isolated case—there are too many others like him. It is crucial that struggling students get help before the effects of failure and shame further complicate the situation.

Unhappy Endings

Dyslexia should not be ignored. If it is, the consequences can be serious. In such cases, school failure and lifelong illiteracy frequently result. The following statistics remind us why society cannot afford to forget these young people:

- *35 percent of students with untreated learning disabilities become high school dropouts.*
- *62 percent of students with untreated learning disabilities remain unemployed one year following their high-school graduation.*
- *60 percent of adults who cannot read were found to have undetected or untreated learning disabilities.*

Four

Getting Help

Derek used to hate school. "I'd think of any excuse not to go and made up all kinds of illnesses. Once I heard that you can make your temperature go up by eating an orange peel. I found out the hard way that it isn't true, but I was desperate.

"At first I'd only willingly go to school on P.E. (physical education) days. I was good in sports and that kind of made up for the rest of school. But as I got older, it just got worse. I could hardly read and school was all about reading. That's why I hated it so much.

"I didn't want anybody to know how hard reading was for me. It was too embarrassing. But after a while I was sent for testing. I didn't want to be tested because I thought I'd have to read to do it but my parents made me go anyway. About a week later they found out the truth and so did I. I wasn't dumb like everyone said. I was dyslexic.

"My parents ended up putting me in a special school. I didn't want to go there either but then I thought that it couldn't be much worse than where I was. The new school wasn't so bad. My class was small and the teacher spent a lot of time with me. Get this—I was one of the best readers there. That might not be saying much but they really helped me. Two years later I was back at my old school. Only now I didn't need to make up stories to stay home."

Making Changes

Many students dramatically improve once they receive the proper help. Students with dyslexia may need different levels of assistance, depending on the severity of the problem. Each case is different. At times, modifying, or changing, standard teaching methods can be beneficial. In a traditional classroom setting, the teacher lectures to a group of young people who sit quietly while focusing on the new material being presented. Afterward, work may be assigned to enable the students to apply what they've learned. They may be expected to complete the assignment before going to their next class. This can often be an extremely stressful situation for young people with dyslexia. Frequently, they are unable to make out many of the words in the assignment. Being expected to finish before the end of class only adds to the pressure and feelings of inadequacy they are likely to experience.

Students with dyslexia often profit from instruction in a language program that stresses, instead, an understanding of the letter-sound system. In many instances, repeatedly going over the material using a multi-sensory teaching method can be helpful. In this multi-sensory approach, the links between what is seen, what is heard, and what is written are emphasized. This means that teachers try to involve the different senses in reading and writing. They

Students with dyslexia often profit from instruction in a language program that stresses an understanding of the letter-sound system.

stress the connection between the sound of the letter and the written symbol. So, instead of just copying a letter off the board, students will write the letter while saying its sound. Using this method, very young children might form the letters out of clay while singing the alphabet. Other teachers prefer using letters made out of precut sandpaper. They have their students run their fingers over the rough side of the sandpaper. Learning this way, the students actually touch the letter while seeing it and hearing its sound.

Some students with dyslexia attend special-education classes that are geared to meet their needs. Public-school systems are required to provide special-education classes, and many private schools offer these as well. There are also private schools that only educate children with various learning disabilities or emotional problems. These schools exist to serve special-needs children and offer a broad range of services in this area.

Special Education Teachers

Within public school systems, special education teachers may play a vital role in helping students with dyslexia. Even when not working with the students themselves, they frequently advise classroom teachers on the following:

- *Modifying or altering the curriculum to meet the student's special needs.*
- *Suggesting supplementary aids and services that might be used by students with dyslexia.*
- *Identifying the best way to test a student with dyslexia to be sure that he or she has absorbed the material presented.*

Other times, a student's dyslexia may be mild enough for that person to be mainstreamed (remain in the same classroom with the majority of the other students). In these instances, changes or accommodations can be made for these students to help them learn as well as to keep up with the rest of the class. Often, tutors, specially trained in teaching learning-disabled students, assist such young people.

Other factors can contribute to the school success of a student with dyslexia as well. Whenever possible, these students should be seated near the front of the classroom where they are better able to focus and less likely to be distracted. At times, photocopying another student's or the teacher's notes is useful. This allows the student to listen more carefully in class rather than struggle with taking notes. Some schools have found it helpful to assign such students a "study buddy." The study buddy is a person in their class who goes over tests and class assignments with them. At times, students with dyslexia are also urged to study with a partner for tests or be part of a study group that meets regularly. In addition, review sheets and study guides can be valuable aids.

Accommodations are also often made for students with dyslexia when tests are scheduled. In some cases, they are given more time to complete their exams. The form of testing used may also differ. Often students with dyslexia do better on essay tests than on multiple-choice exams. That's because it may be difficult for some of them to recognize words taken out of context. Many people with dyslexia also feel that oral instead of written exams offer a truer reflection of their knowledge. Depending on the circumstances, schools may offer a choice of test options.

Special accommodations are also made for students with dyslexia who are going on to college. With so many colleges requiring students to take the SAT or the American College Testing (ACT) Assessment Exam in applying for admission, the law requires that appropriate modifications be made for students with dyslexia. These may include extending the time given to complete the test and working from a large-print or audiocassette version of the text. To receive these accommodations, the student's learning disability must be documented by a qualified professional.

Technological Advances

Technology can also be helpful to students with dyslexia. Books on tape are useful resources for students who have trouble reading. Many students with dyslexia also receive permission to tape class lectures. They can listen to these when studying after school. Some students use headphones

College Bound

Today, large numbers of young people with dyslexia go on to college. Many colleges and universities have special-education labs that feature the latest technology. There are other helpful options offered to learning-disabled students as well. Students with dyslexia may be given more time to take exams, a separate room in which to take the tests, and a transcriber to write down their answers for them. Schools do not regard these aids as special privileges; the educational institutions simply want students with dyslexia to be able to fairly compete. Dr. Jennifer C. Zvi, a learning-disability specialist with California State University at Northridge, says, "All we are doing is leveling the playing field, allowing them [students with dyslexia] to compete with their non-disabled peers on an equal level."

and listen to the tapes when they are jogging, gardening, or walking the dog.

Computers are invaluable aids to numerous students with dyslexia. Many who have trouble writing generally find it easier to type on a computer. They learn to proof their work, and they always use the computer to check their spelling. Besides using computers for homework, sometimes students with dyslexia type their test answers on laptop computers brought to class.

In addition, some rely on Kurzweil 3000, computer software that can assist students with learning disabilities. Used with a computer, it "reads" (out loud) textbooks, pamphlets, articles, and other materials a college student might need to study. The students can scan the printed material and have it read back at a speed that is comfortable for them. Students can also write their own papers using Kurzweil 3000 and hear what they've written read back to them. The software offers the student further guidance by providing spelling and word choices. The latest version of Kurzweil 3000 allows users to download information from the Internet and have it scanned and read back to them.

High-Tech Help

Today, there are many new technological advances to assist students with dyslexia. Among them is a type of computer software known as textHELP. Here, a small box appears on the user's word-processing screen that provides words the person can use without having to spell them. In addition, some people with dyslexia use a device known as a "reading pen" to assist them when they come across words they don't know. This small battery-operated, pen-shaped scanner contains a dictionary. Users simply run the pen across the word they are having trouble reading. The pen will "say" the word out loud, which the user hears through a small earpiece.

Getting Organized

Being disorganized can lead to chaos for any student, but it's even worse if the student has dyslexia. These young people need to establish a homework schedule early on in the school year and stick to it. It is important they make the most of their study time. In doing so, many students with dyslexia have benefited from following these tips for getting organized:

Write down essential information. It's not a good idea to rely on memory to recall class assignments, sports practices, or other school activities. Making lists and jotting down reminders can be helpful as well.

Keep two calendars. A pocket or electronic calendar should be kept with the individual to record appointments throughout the day. After returning home, this information should be transferred to a large wall calendar. The wall calendar should be kept in a place where it can be easily seen. It's best to check it every morning and evening. Some people use different-colored ink on their calendars to reflect their priorities. Essential appointments or things that must be done first are written in red.

Study in a quiet place. The television, radio, and CD player should always be turned off during homework hours. It's best not to check e-mail or take phone calls from friends then either.

Dyslexia and ADHD—They Don't Always Go Together

Many people think that children diagnosed with dyslexia also have attention deficit hyperactivity disorder (ADHD). This isn't so, however. While dyslexia is considered a learning disability, ADHD is a behavioral disorder. Children with ADHD exhibit behaviors that can interfere with their school performance. Although about 12 to 24 percent of individuals with dyslexia also have ADHD, the two don't always go together. The International Dyslexia Association notes that "one is not the cause of the other."

Like dyslexia, ADHD is believed to be genetically based and seems to run in families. If one person in a family has ADHD, there's a 25 to 35 percent chance that at least one other family member will have the disorder as well.

ADHD is largely characterized by being easily distracted, having poor impulse control, and being physically restless. According to the *Diagnostic and Statistical Manual of Mental Health Disorders*, a person with ADHD frequently exhibits the following symptoms:

- has difficulty paying attention to tasks

- seems not to listen when spoken to directly

- fails to follow directions fully and accurately

- loses or forgets things

- feels restless

- fidgets with hands and feet or appears squirmish

- runs or climbs excessively

- talks excessively

- blurts out answers before hearing the whole question

- has difficulty waiting for his or her turn

It is important to remember that the nature and severity of ADHD vary greatly among people. Not everyone has all the symptoms listed above. Symptoms can also differ in intensity from mild to severe.

Young people with ADHD often have trouble in school. It's hard for them to concentrate on what the teacher is saying. They easily become bored and begin talking to their classmates or just fooling around. Sometimes they distract other students near them so no

Dyslexia and ADHD—They Don't Always Go Together *(Continued)*

one gets any work done. Students with ADHD frequently forget to turn their homework in on time or to bring all the items they need to school.

While school presents special challenges for students with ADHD, in many situations these can be overcome. Fortunately, ADHD can be treated. Children with this disorder frequently benefit from behavior-therapy sessions in which they learn techniques to improve how they act in school. Counseling to deal with the emotional effects of having ADHD can be helpful, too. In some cases, medications, such as Ritalin, have also proven effective.

Make good use of library resources. Many libraries have substantial collections of books on tape. Often large-print materials are available as well; some people with dyslexia find these easier to use. Other needed items can sometimes be borrowed from libraries located elsewhere using interlibrary loans.

Break down tasks into small segments. Major projects or assignments are sometimes hard to handle but nevertheless can be done. In these situations, it's important to start early rather than wait until the last minute. It's wise to break down the work into reasonable sections and tackle one segment at a time. Starting computer files for the various segments can help keep things in order, too.

Boosting Self-Esteem

Sandra, who is dyslexic, always had a flair for painting. Though she struggled through her language arts classes, she took first place in art shows and later in life became a successful illustrator of children's books. Looking back on her days as a student, she said, "I don't know what I would have done if my parents hadn't given me art lessons and praised my work. Being good at something helped me feel better about my battle with the written word."

No matter how special they are, it's sometimes hard for young individuals with dyslexia to remember their good qualities. To help boost their self-esteem, they need to zero in on their strong points. It is important for them to remember what they can do well when faced with new challenges. Students with dyslexia should try to build on their strengths. That means finding activities that tap their true potential and allow them to shine. If the person is an artist, he or she can join an art club or take an art class. Those who do well in sports can try out for a sports team. Individuals who are good at interacting with people might volunteer at a hospital or day-care center.

Students with dyslexia should try to build on their strengths. That means finding activities that tap their true potential and allow them to shine.

People with dyslexia also need to identify their weak areas and find out what help is available to them. It's important for them to learn new techniques or strategies that could help them meet daily challenges. Finally, students with dyslexia should learn as much as they can about this learning disability. This can help them better understand what they may be going through at times. It will also help them to best explain their needs to others. There is an old saying, "any road up the mountain." It means that the way to success is not always an easy or direct path. People have to try different ways to get where they want to go and to make their dreams come true. No one with dyslexia should ever forget that.

Individuals with dyslexia may not ever be like the majority of people surrounding them. But being different frequently means being able to bring a fresh perspective to a situation—and that's a wonderful quality. People with dyslexia have become doctors, lawyers, artists, actors, singers, and scientists and have found success in countless other professions. Throughout history, they have made important contributions to society. It's likely that they'll continue to do so in the future.

Glossary

• Attention Deficit Hyperactivity Disorder (ADHD): a behavioral
• disorder characterized by restlessness, poor impulse control,
• and an inability to pay attention
•
•
• behavioral therapy: a form of therapy that teaches ways to
• overcome negative habits and/or actions and encourages
• positive ones
•
•
• compensate: to make up for something or counterbalance
•
•
• comprehension: understanding
•
•
• conscientious: making certain that something is done
• properly and thoroughly

diagnose: the process of determining what disorder or disease someone has

dyslexic dysgraphia: a processing problem that interferes with the ability to write

dyspraxia: a disorder that affects motor skills development (movement) which can also negatively influence various aspects of learning and school performance

genes: the basic unit of heredity that determines a person's traits as passed from parent to offspring

genetics: relating to the origin or development of something

illiteracy: the inability to read or write

information processing disorders: conditions in which people have difficulty effectively using the information they collect through their senses

mainstream: the process of placing a learning-disabled student in the same class as other students

modification: to change something slightly

multisensory method: a technique that combines seeing, hearing, and writing to help dyslexic students with their language skills

neuropathologist: a doctor whose specialty is the nervous system

phonemes: the smallest units of sound that make up words

phonetics: a branch of language study concerned with the production of speech sounds and their representation in writing

psychologist: a specialist who studies human behavior, especially mental and behavioral characteristics

Ritalin (methylphenidate, MPH): a medication that is sometimes used to treat ADHD

transcriber: someone who writes words from notes or shorthand

Further Resources

Books

Coman, Marcia J. *What You Need to Know about Developing Study Skills, Taking Notes & Tests, Using Dictionaries & Libraries.* Lincolnwood, Ill.: National Textbook Company, 1991.

Connelly, Elizabeth Russell. *A World Upside Down and Backwards: Reading and Learning Disorders.* Broomall, Pa: Chelsea House, 1999.

Cummings, Rhoda Woods and Gary L. Fisher. *The School Survival Guide for Kids with LD (Learning Differences).* Minneapolis: Free Spirit Publishers, 1991.

Donnelly, Karen. *Coping with Dyslexia.* New York: Rosen Publishing, 2000.

Fisher, Gary L. *The Survival Guide for Kids with LD (Learning Differences).* Minneapolis: Free Spirit Publishers, 1990.

Gehret, Jeanne. *The Don't-Give-Up Kid and Learning Differences.* Fairport, NY: Verbal Images Press, 1996.

Levine, Melvin D. *All Kinds of Minds: A Young Student's Book about Learning Abilities and Learning Disorders.* Cambridge, Mass.: Educators Publishing Service, 1993.

Levine, Melvin D. *Keeping a Head in School: A Student's Book about Learning Abilities and Learning Disorders.* Cambridge, Mass.: Educators Publishing Service, 1991.

Moragne, Wendy. *Dyslexia.* Brookfield, Conn.: Millbrook Press, 1997.

Porterfield, Kay Marie. *Straight Talk about Learning Disabilities.* New York: Facts on File, 1999.

Stern, Judith M. *Many Ways to Learn: Young People's Guide to Learning Disabilities.* Washington, D.C.: Magination Press, 1996.

Online Sites and Organizations

The International Dyslexia Association
Chester Building, Ste. 382
8600 LaSalle Rd.
Baltimore, MD 21286
(410) 296-0232
www.interdys.org
Educators, teens, children, parents, adults, and college students can find information about dyslexia on this web site.

Learning Disabilities Association of America
4156 Library Rd.
Pittsburgh, PA 15234
(412) 341-1515
www.ldanatl.org
This web site offers fact sheets as well as links providing more information about videos, government agencies, audiotapes, and other resources about learning disabilities.

National Center for Learning Disabilities
381 Park Ave. South, Ste. 1401
New York, NY 10016
(888) 575-7373
www.ld.org
Visitors to this web site can peruse a variety of fact sheets about various aspects of learning disabilities, as well as news about the latest research regarding education techniques.

Hello Friend
The Ennis William Cosby Foundation
P.O. Box 4061
Santa Monica, CA 90411
www.hellofriend.com
The Ennis William Cosby Foundation helps young people to celebrate their gifts and reach their potential. The web site provides links to relevant organizations, articles, newsletters, and events about dyslexia and other language-based learning differences.

Schwab Learning

1650 S. Amphlett Blvd., Ste. 300

San Mateo, CA 94402

(650) 655-2410

www.SchwabLearning.org/SparkTop

Created expressly for kids 8-12 who learn differently, this engaging site offers plenty of interactive content as well as audio.

LD Resources

202 Lake Rd.

New Preston, CT 06777

(860) 868-3214

www.ldresources.com

This web site includes articles about various aspects of learning disabilities and also allows people to participate in discussion forums.

Index

About the Author

Award-winning author **Elaine Landau** received a bachelor's degree in English and journalism from New York University and a master's degree in library and information science from Pratt Institute. She worked as a newspaper reporter, children's book editor, and a youth services librarian before becoming a full-time writer. She has written more than two hundred nonfiction books for children and young adults. She lives in Miami, Florida, with her husband, Norman, and their son, Michael.